MIGRATION
Incredible Animal Journeys

Mike Unwin

ILLUSTRATED BY

Jenni Desmond

BLOOMSBURY
CHILDREN'S BOOKS
NEW YORK LONDON OXFORD NEW DELHI SYDNEY

CONTENTS

ANIMALS ON THE MOVE

Imagine being a baby swallow in Europe in the autumn. Just a few weeks ago you left your nest for the first time. Now, before you are even two months old, you have to fly thousands of miles—all the way to Africa.

And your challenge doesn't end there. Next spring, when you are old enough to make your own nest, you will have to fly all the way back to Europe again. In fact, every year, for the rest of your life, you will make that same journey to and from Africa.

Swallows are not the only long-distance travelers. Many different animals around the world make similar journeys—crossing mountains, deserts, and oceans along the way. These journeys are called migrations, and they happen in many different ways: while birds fly through the air, elephants trek across the land and turtles swim through the sea.

Animals migrate because their environment changes with the seasons. They travel to new places where they can find food and give birth safely. Along the way, they must survive harsh weather and hungry predators. It may sound exhausting, but if these travelers stayed put they would not be able to survive. This book follows the migration journeys of twenty different animals around the world. Each has its own amazing story to tell.

A WHALE OF A JOURNEY

A baby humpback whale sticks close to its mother as they move through the deep blue ocean. At just six months old, this baby already weighs as much as an elephant. But it still needs its mother: the two have a long journey ahead. Along the way, she will protect her baby and provide milk to help it grow bigger and stronger.

The mother gave birth during winter in the warm Pacific Ocean, near Australia. Many humpback whales gathered here, all looking after their babies. They didn't feed. Instead, they lived off the fat that their bodies had put on during the previous summer.

Now the whales are hungry again. They are heading south to the Antarctic, where they will find their food. It will be summer there when they arrive. The cold Antarctic waters will be full of tiny, shrimp-like creatures called krill, which whales love to eat. They will feed for about six months, gulping down krill in huge mouthfuls. The baby will learn how to do this, and soon it will start building up the thick layer of blubber that it needs to keep out the cold.

Around April, the humpback whales will return north. The youngsters will have grown large enough to fend for themselves. In the warm Pacific they will splash and play, whacking the water with their tails and sometimes leaping clear of the surface.

At ten years old, our baby humpback whale will be full-grown. For the rest of its life it will migrate every year between the warm Pacific and the cold Antarctic. It may travel more than 15,000 miles a year. That's the longest swim of any animal on Earth.

Humpback whales grow up to 60 feet long.
They spend winter in warm oceans around
the world, where they have their calves.
In summer they migrate to polar regions,
where they feed.

ICE MARCH

Brrrr! It's the middle of the Antarctic. All you can see for miles is ice. But look closer. A line of figures is trooping over the frozen terrain. From a distance they look like people. But soon you can see that they're penguins. Each follows the one in front.

These are emperor penguins, the biggest of the world's penguins and the only ones that breed in the middle of the Antarctic. Now winter is approaching. They have left the sea behind and are traveling inland to their breeding grounds. It's a journey of nearly 60 miles. Sometimes they rest their tired feet by flopping onto their tummies and tobogganing over the ice.

When the penguins reach their breeding grounds, each pair finds its own place. The female lays a single egg, then she returns to the sea to go fishing. While she is away, the male looks after the egg by balancing it on his warm feet. All the males in the breeding colony huddle together during the icy winter storms. Once the eggs hatch, each cares for his chick, keeping it snug under the soft, warm feathers of his tummy.

After two cold months, the female returns with fish. The parents then take turns feeding their growing chick until December (summer in the Antarctic), when the youngsters make their own march to the sea. Here they learn to feed themselves. After four years they are grown up and ready to breed. Now they too will migrate inland, making the same journey as their parents.

The emperor penguin is the world's largest penguin. It lives only in Antarctica. It fishes in the sea during summer then migrates inland in winter to breed.

CARIBOU CROSSING

Splash! The caribou steps off into the icy water and starts to swim. A baby, close behind, hesitates briefly, then plunges in to join its mother. Together the two deer make their way across the river. They hold their heads above the surface while, down below, their long legs kick hard.

The strong current carries the swimmers a little way downstream from where they started, but soon they are clambering out on the bank. They shake the water from their thick fur and step forward. Another river safely crossed.

These two caribou are not alone. Thousands have already crossed the river and thousands more are following behind. Altogether there are more than 100,000 animals. They have been traveling for weeks, crossing many rivers on their long migration south.

Caribou are wild reindeer that live in the northernmost parts of North America. They spend summer on the open Arctic plains, called tundra, then migrate south in huge herds to spend winter in the cover of the forests.

The caribou's epic journey started along the shore of the Arctic Ocean, where they spent the summer. Here the females gave birth. Now they are heading inland toward the forests: the trees will help protect them when winter comes. They'll be able to dig through the snow with their hooves and find enough moss and lichen to eat. Then in spring they'll head back toward the ocean.

As each caribou climbs out of the water it joins the others who have already crossed. The herd gathers together again. The animals are exhausted but they do not rest. They know that bad weather is on the way and that other dangers, such as wolves, lie in wait. There is no time to waste. Soon they are moving again, always sticking close together.

POLE TO POLE

It's the middle of the Arctic summer, up near the North Pole. The clock shows midnight but the sun is still shining on the sea. An Arctic tern flutters over the waves. Spying a shoal of silvery fish, it swoops down and snatches one in its sharp red beak. Just what it needs to feed its hungry chicks! It flies back toward its nest on land with its wriggling catch in its beak.

This is a busy season for Arctic terns. During summer in polar regions, the sun hardly sets. This means that the terns can keep fishing for twenty-four hours a day, catching plenty of food for their young. Other Arctic animals are also busy: polar bears stalk seals across the ice, while whales sieve huge mouthfuls of plankton from the cold water.

During winter, though, the sea freezes over and it's dark all day long. Seabirds migrate south for warmth and food. The Arctic tern travels farther than any other—all the way down the Atlantic Ocean to the Antarctic. While it's winter in the Arctic, it's summer in the Antarctic. So with twenty-four hours of daylight there, the tern can keep fishing as long as it likes.

The Arctic tern's epic journey from pole to pole is the longest migration made by any animal. It can travel up to 60,000 miles every year. This means that over its lifetime one individual may fly as far as four round-trips to the moon. In a migration Olympics, this amazing little bird would definitely win gold!

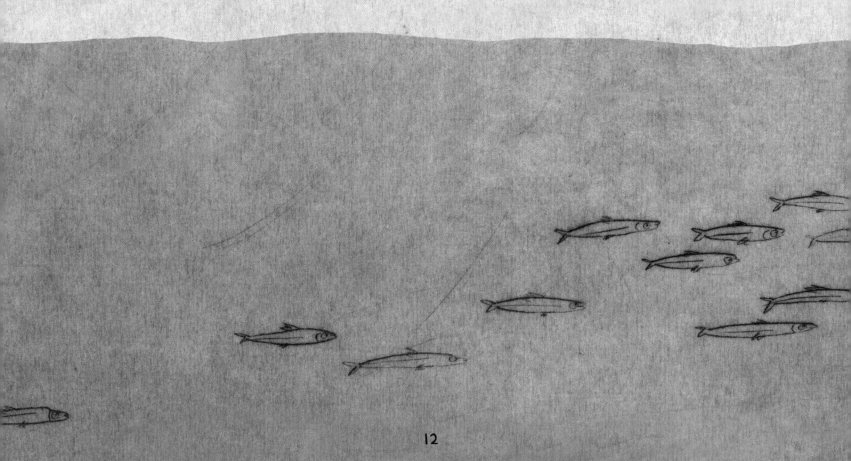

The Arctic tern breeds on coasts all around the Arctic
Circle: in Europe, Asia, and North America. Many nest
together in large colonies beside the sea. Every winter they
migrate south to the Antarctic.

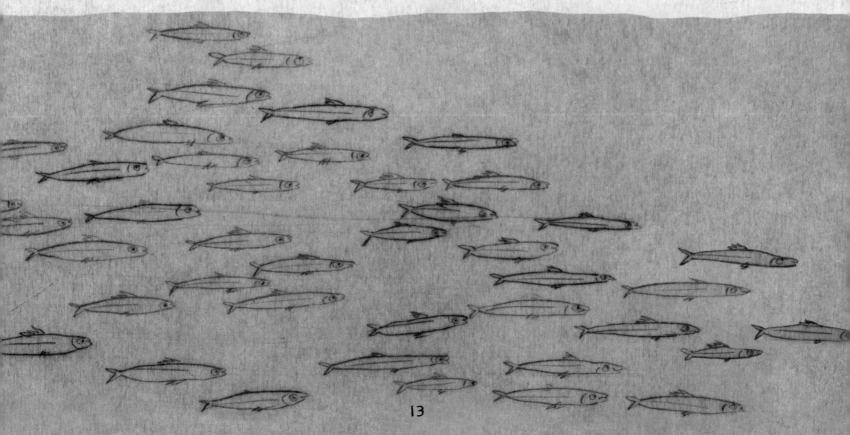

FORESTS OF FLUTTER

High in a mountain forest in Mexico, the air is dancing with butterflies. A confetti of peach-colored wings flutters in the winter sunlight. Thousands more cluster on the branches of the oyamel fir trees, forming a thick butterfly blanket. Counting them is impossible. There are millions.

These handsome butterflies are called monarchs. Every year they gather to spend winter in a few special Mexican forests. To get there, they migrate all the way from the United States, where they grew from caterpillars. Some have flown from as far as southern Canada, traveling more than 3,000 miles.

Winter in the northern US and Canada gets very cold. That's why the monarchs head south. In these Mexican mountains, they find a safe place to roost. They huddle together to keep warm and save energy, though any disturbance may send thousands fluttering into the air for a while.

In spring, the butterflies will lay their eggs. The new monarchs will then start to migrate north, laying more eggs along the way. By July—after three generations of monarchs have hatched, laid their eggs, and died—the fourth generation will reach its northernmost summer home. These are the monarchs that live the longest. In late September they will start the long migration south to Mexico. Then in spring they will lay their eggs and die.

Migrating monarchs can travel up to 60 miles per day, using strong air currents to help them along. It's an amazing journey for an insect that can weigh less than a paper clip! Scientists don't fully understand how butterflies can find their way to a hidden forest, thousands of miles away, that they have never seen before.

The monarch butterfly is a large butterfly that breeds in North America and migrates south to winter in Mexico, where it is warmer. No individual butterfly completes the two-way migration: it takes four generations, which complete their life cycles along the way.

TRAVELING DANCERS

The whooping crane is a tall,
very rare bird that breeds in
forests in Canada and the
northern US. It migrates south
every year to spend winter
on the coast of the Gulf of
Mexico, in the southern US.

Two tall white birds leap into the air, wings outstretched. They bounce up and down, circling each other, stretching their long necks high, then bowing their heads low. It's like a feathered ballet, and the music comes from their high bugling calls. Others soon join the chorus.

These birds are whooping cranes. They have gathered in marshlands beside the Gulf of Mexico, on the south coast of the United States. They arrived in autumn and spent the winter here, but now spring is approaching and it's time to leave.

The dancers are a male and a female. They have nested together for several years, and this dance helps keep them close. Other cranes are dancing too. Each pair knows that it's time to build a nest and start raising a family. But first they must return to their breeding grounds in the north.

At nearly 5 feet tall, whooping cranes are the tallest birds in North America. They are also one of the rarest—in 1941 there were only twenty-three left, including two in zoos. Conservationists have worked hard to protect them and today there are around 400 in the wild.

Every year, the cranes migrate between their breeding grounds in the northern US and Canada, and their wintering grounds in the south—a journey of 2,500 miles. To help show young cranes the way, conservationists fly alongside them in an ultralight aircraft!

Once they reach the north, the cranes build their nest in a wild boggy area in the middle of a forest. Here they raise their single chick. Today this forest receives special protection. And as the cranes' numbers increase every year, so the ballet show keeps getting bigger and better.

OFF TO AFRICA

Twitter, twitter, twitter! Swallows are lining up on the wires, looking like musical notes on a staff. It's autumn: the first leaves are falling; the days are growing shorter and the nights chillier. The birds are restless. They can't stay here through the cold, dark English winter. It's time to head to Africa.

For a few more days the flock will keep feeding, building up strength. Then, when the wind changes, they will all leave together. The journey ahead is daunting: they must cross seas, mountains, and the huge Sahara Desert, traveling more than 6,000 miles in just five weeks. Fierce storms and hungry predators lie in wait. Not every swallow will make it.

So why do swallows risk this perilous journey? It's all about insects. These agile little birds are experts at catching the flying bugs that fill the summer skies. They dart about over fields and ponds, snapping up their prey and taking it back to their nest–often in an old building–where their hungry chicks wait.

In winter the insects are gone. The young swallows would have nothing to eat if they stayed. They must head off somewhere warmer.

By the end of October, most swallows have reached southern Africa. This marks the end of their journey. They swarm across the savannah, catching as many insects as they need. For four or five months they stay in Africa. But by March it is time to build their nests again, so they head back to Europe. Many return to the very building in which they were born.

The barn swallow is a small, insect-eating bird that breeds in the northern hemisphere. It often lives around farms, where it builds nests of mud in old buildings.

FLIGHT OF THE DRAGONS

Imagine: You're relaxing on a tropical island when a dragonfly lands on your flip-flop. You wiggle your toe and it flies off with a rustle of wings. But another one takes its place. It's as long as your middle finger, with see-through wings and a golden body. You look up: there are lots more in the air, darting and hovering, landing on chairs and tables.

The globe skimmer dragonfly does indeed skim all over the globe. Every fall, huge swarms appear on the Maldives, a chain of islands in the middle of the Indian Ocean. A few weeks later they appear in the Seychelles, islands farther west. Then by December they appear on the coast of eastern Africa. For years people wondered where these insects came from and how they got there.

Scientists now know the globe skimmer dragonfly migrates all the way from India to eastern Africa. It hops from island to island in a southwesterly direction across the Indian Ocean, traveling at a height of over 3,000 feet. Tropical winds help blow it along. They also carry rain, so whenever the dragonflies reach land there is fresh water in which to lay their eggs. The eggs hatch, and in just six weeks the larvae develop into young dragonflies that continue the journey.

In spring, a new generation hatches in eastern Africa and migrates all the way back to India. In one year, over the course of four generations, this dragonfly has made a round-trip of over 6,000 miles. This is the longest migration of any insect. Countless millions make the journey. Along the way, they provide vital food for falcons, bee-eaters, and other birds that migrate alongside them.

The globe skimmer dragonfly is the
most widespread dragonfly in the
world. Its migration from India to
eastern Africa and back again, over
four generations, is the longest of
any insect.

SHOAL SURVIVORS

Imagine: It's June, and you're a seabird flying high above the sunny coastline of South Africa. The blue ocean sparkles below. Along the horizon stretches the distant shore. But what's that? There's a dark stain on the sea. The lower you fly, the bigger it seems to get, stretching for four to nine miles along the coast. At first it looks like spilled oil, but soon you can see that the stain is moving, heading slowly east. Aha! It's not oil but fish—millions and millions of them, all swimming in one enormous shoal.

South Africa's famous "sardine run" is one of the world's biggest migrations. These little silvery fish, also known as pilchards, gather every May in the cold waters off South Africa's Cape before moving northeastward toward the warmer Indian Ocean coast of Mozambique.

This enormous shoal provides vital food for many animals. The hunters soon arrive: thousands of dolphins and sharks attack from under water, while gannets dive down from above. Even whales appear, swallowing huge mouthfuls. Gradually the huge shoal breaks up into many smaller shoals, each one getting smaller.

Scientists don't fully understand why the pilchards migrate. But they know that these fish like cold water. Their journey follows a cold current that flows east every winter around South Africa's coast. We don't know how many sardines finish their journey, where they end up, or how they return. Nobody has ever seen them on their way back. But we do know that, next May, the sardine run will happen all over again.

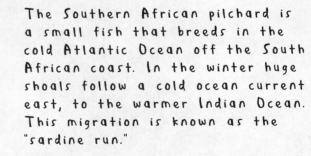

The Southern African pilchard is a small fish that breeds in the cold Atlantic Ocean off the South African coast. In the winter huge shoals follow a cold ocean current east, to the warmer Indian Ocean. This migration is known as the "sardine run."

WANDERING WINGS

In the middle of the Southern Ocean, thousands of miles from land, a storm is raging. Fierce gusts whip up the waves and rain lashes the heaving sea. Through the wild weather comes a big white bird. Gliding on enormous wings, it tilts low over the waves— so low its wing tips nearly touch the surface.

The bird is a young wandering albatross. It doesn't mind the storm: the wild wind and waves are its home. Many months have passed since it last saw land. It is an amazing flyer. At over ten feet across, its wings stretch as wide as two kitchen tables laid end to end.

The wandering albatross gets its name for a good reason. Unlike other birds, it doesn't migrate from one place to another and back again. Instead it wanders the ocean in huge circles, constantly searching for food.

Five to ten years ago this young albatross left the small rocky island where it was born. Ever since then it has been wandering, covering more than 60,000 miles a year—over a quarter of the distance from the Earth to the Moon. Never once has it touched land, though the birds often roost on the surface of the water.

In a year or two, when the youngster is ready to breed, it will return to find a mate on the rocky island where it was born. The pair will build a nest of mud, grass, and moss. The female will lay one big white egg and, when this hatches, the parents will look after the fluffy chick for nearly nine months. When it is ready, the youngster will launch out into the sea breeze to start a wandering life of its own.

The wandering albatross is a huge seabird that breeds on islands in the southern hemisphere. It circles the oceans in search of food. Young birds travel for many years before they return to land to breed.

RIVER OF CRABS

Stop the car, quick! There's a red river flowing right across the road. You'll have to wait.

But look closer. It's not water: it's crabs. Big red ones. There are thousands of them. They pour across the road in an army of pincers, then scuttle down the bank on the other side, heading for the sea.

You're on Christmas Island, northwest of Australia. These are Christmas Island red crabs. Most of the year they live in forests at the center of the island, sheltering from the hot sun in cool, damp burrows. But at the start of the rainy season, around November, they migrate to the sea to lay their eggs. Millions move together.

The journey takes about one week. The males set off first and are later joined by the females. On the beaches the males dig new burrows in the sand, then they mate. After mating, the males return to the forest. The females remain for two weeks, waiting for the right time to lay their eggs. At the first high tide they release their eggs into the sea.

The tiny baby crabs, called larvae, hatch immediately and are swept out to sea in clouds. Here they feed and grow until, after three or four weeks, they are big enough—about the size of a pea—to return to land. It takes them nine days to reach the center of the island, where they hide among rocks and logs. After four years they are ready to make their first migration back to the sea.

Roads are dangerous for migrating crabs. But Christmas Islanders have built special fences and underpasses to help them get across, and the red river keeps on flowing.

Christmas Island red crabs are found only on Christmas Island and two nearby islands in the Indian Ocean. They live in burrows inland. Every November millions migrate to the coast and lay their eggs in the sea.

HUMMING OVER OCEANS

Try flapping your arms like a bird. Easy, you think? Now try doing it fifty times in one second. Impossible! But that's how a ruby-throated hummingbird flies. It flaps its wings so fast they make a humming sound, like an insect. This helps it to hover in midair, while it sips the sweet nectar from a flower with its long tongue. It can even fly backward.

Amazingly, this tiny bird, which weighs less than a sugar lump, can fly 500 miles across the ocean. Imagine how many flaps that must take! Every spring, it leaves its tropical winter home in Central America and flies north to North America. And to arrive quickly, it takes the most direct route: straight across the wide, blue Gulf of Mexico.

The ruby-throated hummingbird is a tiny bird that feeds on nectar from flowers. It breeds in North America, as far north as Canada, but migrates south in winter to tropical Central America.

Along the way, this tireless traveler may make a quick stop, perhaps perching for a while on a fishing boat or an oil rig. But there is no time to lose—it has to find the best place to build its tiny cup-shaped nest before another hummingbird gets there first.

By April, most ruby-throated hummingbirds have reached their northern homes. They settle down to nest in woods, parks, and gardens. Spring flowers provide plenty of nectar, giving them energy to raise their family. Parents also catch insects as extra food for their hungry, growing chicks.

By August, the chicks have left the nest and are busy buzzing about on their new fast-flapping wings. They must learn quickly—in September they will have to set off on the long journey south.

OVER THE MOUNTAINS

Imagine: You're high in the Himalayas, all alone, when you hear distant voices. The sound carries over the snowy slopes and echoes down the frozen canyons. It grows steadily louder, as though a crowd is approaching. But nobody lives up here. What on earth can it be?

Then you notice a long line of birds winging toward you. Suddenly that mysterious sound makes sense: it's not people you can hear, but a flock of geese. The line stretches out in a straggly V shape. Soon the birds are passing directly overhead, necks stretched out and wings beating steadily. They honk to keep in touch with each other, like flying trumpets.

These birds are bar-headed geese–named for the smart black stripes on their heads. In summer they nest on lakes in central Asia, each pair raising from three to eight youngsters. Then in autumn, when the weather turns cold, they migrate south to India. To reach their destination, they must fly over the Himalayas, the highest mountains on Earth.

No other bird makes this journey. It is full of danger. At this height, the temperature falls way below freezing and the air is very thin. A special circulation system helps pump oxygen around the birds' bodies to keep them flying. They must also dodge golden eagles, which swoop out to attack them.

Once they reach India, the geese can relax and recover. In the lush, warm wetlands they find plenty of grass to eat, and the youngsters can grow strong. By spring, they will be ready to tackle the mountains again as they return to their breeding grounds in the north.

The bar-headed goose is a large water bird that breeds in Central Asia, mostly in China. In winter it migrates in large flocks to northern India, passing over the Himalayas along the way.

The great white shark is the largest predatory shark. It lives in cool waters around the world, hunting around coasts and islands for large prey such as seals. It migrates across oceans in search of food.

GREAT WHITE WANDERINGS

With a swish of its tail, the great white shark powers through the deep blue depths. This huge ocean fish measures 15 feet long–the length of two cars laid end to end. With teeth that can bite a seal in half, it is one of the scariest predators on the planet. But today it isn't hunting. In fact, it hasn't eaten for weeks. Instead, it is on a journey.

Great white sharks feed mostly around the coast, where their favorite prey is young seals. But the seals don't stay in one place all year round, so the sharks have to move. This individual left the coast of South Africa when the seals vacated their breeding grounds. It is now halfway through an amazing 6,000-mile journey, right across the Indian Ocean to the coast of Australia. When it arrives the seals will be breeding, so there will be plenty of prey to hunt.

In the middle of the ocean it is harder to find food. The great white shark doesn't waste time hunting; instead it gets energy from the store of fat around its liver. It built up this fat by eating lots of seals back in South Africa. While swimming, it saves energy by drifting into the depths, where it is carried slowly forward. To speed up again it swims back to the surface.

Great white sharks probably migrate farther than any other shark. Scientists have learned about their underwater journeys by fixing satellite tags to their fins and using the signals to follow where they go. This shark will not stop traveling until it reaches the coast of Australia. And when it arrives, look out, seals!

JUMBO JOURNEYS

In the dry Kalahari region of southern Africa, it has not rained for six months. The grass is yellow, the riverbeds are dry, and animals are on the move in search of water. Through the dusty bush comes a herd of elephants. They move in a line, trunks swinging. Nervous babies stick close to their mothers. Out in front is an old female, known as the matriarch. She is in charge.

The matriarch has been traveling back and forth across the Kalahari for fifty years. Her memory holds a perfect map of the land. It tells her where to find food and how to avoid danger. Now she must lead her thirsty herd to water.

She knows just where to go. Every year, as the dry season gets ever hotter, the elephants migrate to a huge wetland called the Okavango. Here they find pools and rivers, with water to drink and lots of greenery to eat. Family groups join together in the migration, forming herds of hundreds.

The elephants are excited when they arrive. They love water: they suck it up in their trunks and squirt it into their mouths. Youngsters wade into the pools, splashing and wallowing. Teenagers have noisy play-fights, scattering the other animals that also come to drink. Even lions get out of the way.

When the rain starts to fall again, the land quickly turns green with new growth. There is food and water everywhere. The big elephant gatherings break up and the family herds head back out into the Kalahari. Each sticks with its matriarch. They will need her to find the way again next year.

The African elephant is the largest land animal in the world. During the dry season, herds migrate large distances to find food and water. Adults may drink 50 gallons a day.

The Pacific salmon is a large fish found in northern parts of the Atlantic and Pacific Oceans. Adults spend most of their life at sea, but migrate to the rivers where they were born to lay their eggs upstream.

SALMON SURGE

Onward and upward! As the river tumbles downstream over rocks and rapids, determined travelers are battling in the opposite direction. Salmon need all their strength to swim against the current. At the rapids they fling their bodies out of the water, sometimes leaping six feet into the air to get across. Nothing seems to stop them.

The salmon are heading for the calm, clear waters farther upstream. Here, each female will lay up to 17,000 eggs on the gravel riverbed. Already these fish have traveled hundreds of miles from the Pacific. After living in the ocean for years, they have now left the sea and returned to the rivers where they were born. This journey will be the last of their lives: once their eggs are laid, the salmon will die.

Not every salmon will make it upriver. Hungry grizzly bears gather along the banks and try to snatch them from the water. These big furry hunters eat salmon every year, to fatten up for winter. Bald eagles fly down to feed on the fish that have died. Nothing goes to waste.

When the eggs hatch, the young salmon—called fry—feed on tiny plankton in the water. They spend at least a few months in the river before swiming down toward the river mouth. Finally, when they are ready for life in salt water, they swim out to sea. Here they live for four years or more, traveling huge distances as they grow bigger. Then one spring they return to the mouth of the river where they were born. Here they will make their final journey: battling upstream to lay their eggs.

FAR AND WIDE
FOR FISH

Splash! The osprey dives feet first into the surf and emerges with a fish clutched in its sharp talons. Flapping hard, the big bird takes off and flies over the beach. It carries its slippery prize to a baobab tree. Now it can dig into its meal.

It's a sunny October morning on the west coast of Africa. This osprey has just flown all the way from Scotland. It was born in May, one of four babies in a big stick nest on top of a Scots pine tree. All summer, the adults looked after their chicks, bringing fresh fish to them every day. The chicks grew bigger and stronger. By August they had learned to fly and catch fish for themselves.

In September the osprey set off alone for Africa, where winter is warmer. Its long journey south took it across the English Channel and over the coast of France and Spain. It flew high over cities and farmland, stopping off at lakes to catch fish. Sometimes it waited a few days for a storm to pass.

Now it is spending winter on this tropical coast, sharing its home with monkeys and other African creatures. Each morning, as local fishermen unload their catch from painted boats, it flies out to make its own catch.

In March the osprey will return north, retracing its journey to Scotland. By April, it will be back near the lake where it was born. As soon as it arrives it will look for a mate. The two birds will then build a nest and start a new family of their own.

The osprey is a large bird of prey that feeds only on fish. Ospreys that breed in northern Europe migrate south every year to spend the winter in Africa.

HOOVES ON THE MOVE

On East Africa's Serengeti plains a distant storm is breaking. The wildebeests stop grazing and lift their heads. Thunder rumbles and lightning flashes on the horizon. Far away, across the big river, rain is falling. By tomorrow new shoots will be peeking up. Soon there will be a carpet of lush, green grass.

Months have passed since the wildebeests last felt rain. The plains where they are standing are bone dry, with hardly any grass left to eat. But they can smell the distant rain. They know they must leave this place and head to where the new grass is growing.

Small groups begin to move. These form larger herds, and soon thousands of hungry wildebeests are on the move. They trudge in long lines that crisscross the dusty ground. Other animals join them: groups of stripy zebras and dainty gazelles. They're all heading toward the rain.

The journey is long and tiring. The travelers stick together, looking out for hunters that might ambush them. Lions lurk behind bushes. Hyenas attack at night.

Eventually the wildebeests reach the river. They gather on the banks, looking for a good place to cross. It's scary: the current is strong and the water is full of huge crocodiles. But when one takes the plunge, the others follow. Soon thousands are leaping in. They must swim with all their strength.

On the other side, the wildebeests find fresh green grazing. Now they can grow plump and healthy again. Mothers give birth to calves: the new grass helps them produce milk for their wobbly youngsters. The calves must grow up quickly because the herds will be on the move again as soon as the rain stops.

The blue wildebeest is an African antelope about the size of a
pony. Big herds live on open plains and eat grass. They migrate
every year to wherever the rain allows new grass to grow.

BATTY FOR FRUIT

Dawn is breaking over Kasanka Forest. But the sky is darkening with countless beating wings–not the feathered wings of birds, but the soft, leathery wings of straw-colored fruit bats. Thousands fill the air, flapping and jostling as they search for roosting spots among the trees.

The bats chatter and screech as they arrive. As each one lands, it grips the branch with its claws and swings around to hang upside down. Once comfortable, it closes its eyes, ready to sleep for the day.

The straw-colored fruit bat is one of Africa's biggest bats, measuring three feet across its wings. It gets its name from its yellowish fur. Every year, millions migrate from central Africa to Kasanka. This small forest in Zambia is no bigger than four football fields, but in November, up to ten million bats make their home here. Some have flown more than 1,000 miles to arrive. It's the farthest migration of any mammal in Africa.

Why do they come? For fruit, of course! In November, Kasanka's trees are groaning with wild mangoes and other juicy treats. The bats set out at sunset and feed all night. As dawn is breaking, they fly back to their roosting trees. Here they find protection from hunters such as fish eagles that might attack them during daylight.

By January, Kasanka's trees are stripped of all their fruit. Now it's time for the bats to leave. They fly back toward central Africa, traveling by night. Nobody knows exactly where they go to. But next year, when the trees are in fruit once again, they'll be back.

The straw-colored fruit bat is one of Africa's largest bats. Large colonies breed across central Africa. They migrate during the rainy season to special places where they can find lots of fruit, such as Kasanka in Zambia.

TURTLE RETURNS

Waves break on a moonlit beach on Ascension Island in the Atlantic Ocean. As the surf retreats, it leaves behind something on the wet sand. At first it looks like a big round rock, but soon it begins to move. It's a green sea turtle. Stretching out two tired flippers, it hauls itself slowly up the beach.

This huge marine reptile weighs as much as two people. It has swum over 1,000 miles to get here. For the last two years it has been feeding near the coast of Brazil, on the other side of the Atlantic, but now it has returned to Ascension to lay its eggs. It knows this beach well–it was born here.

Every year, thousands of green turtles migrate across the Atlantic to breed on Ascension. When they arrive, the males and females gather in the warm waters just offshore. Once the females are ready to lay their eggs,

they go ashore. After dark, each female crawls up to the dry sand at the top of the beach, digs a deep hole with its flippers, and lays around one hundred soft, round eggs. It covers the nest with sand, then returns to the ocean and swims away.

Six to eight weeks later the eggs hatch. The babies, each the size of a tangerine, dig themselves out and scurry down to the surf. For the next twenty years they live at sea, wandering widely as they gradually grow bigger. Their diet changes from tiny animals to sea grass and other marine plants.

Once the youngsters have grown big enough to start breeding, they migrate back to their hatching beaches. Every two or three years, the females arrive to lay more eggs. Some may live to be eighty years old.

Green turtles are large marine reptiles that nest on islands and coastlines in tropical seas around the world. They travel widely as they grow. Then they return to the beaches where they were born to lay their eggs.

ALL AROUND THE WORLD

This map shows all the migration journeys described in this book. Some of the animals in this book also make other journeys that are not shown here.

DID YOU KNOW?

- People have only started to fully understand bird migration in the last 150 years. Scientists once thought swallows hibernated during winter at the bottom of ponds, just as frogs do!
- Humpback whales can hear each other's underwater songs from more than 20 miles away.
- Swifts can spend up to ten months in the air during their migration, feeding and sleeping on the wing and never landing at all.
- Some migrations in the past were bigger than any today. In 1849 a herd of several million springbok (a small antelope) took three days to pass by one town in South Africa.
- Many birds migrate at night: they work out directions from the position of the moon and stars.

MAKING A SAFER WORLD FOR MIGRANTS

Migrating animals face many natural dangers—from wild weather to hungry predators. But today many of the worst dangers are caused by people. Cattle fences in Africa block the way of migrating antelope; whales and other sea creatures become entangled in fishing nets; and hunters trap millions of migrating songbirds.

By cutting down forests, polluting oceans, and draining wetlands, people are also damaging the vital natural habitats through which animals migrate. Today these animals need our help. Migration routes cross many different countries, so governments and conservation organizations across the world must work together to protect the migrants and safeguard the places where they live and travel.

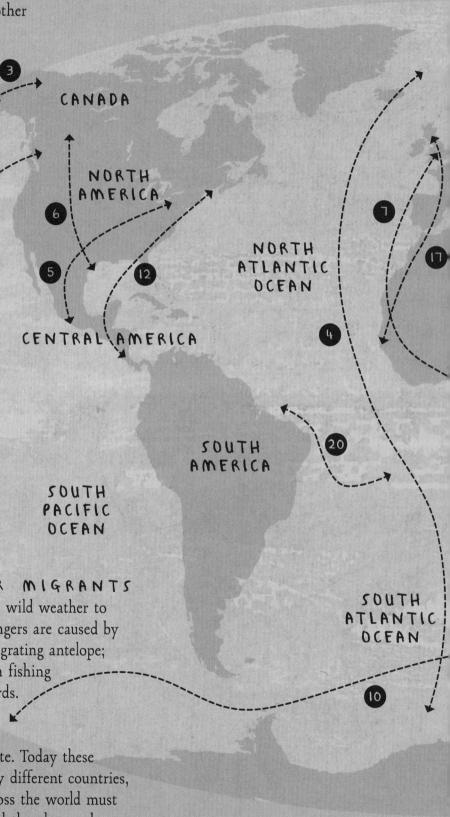

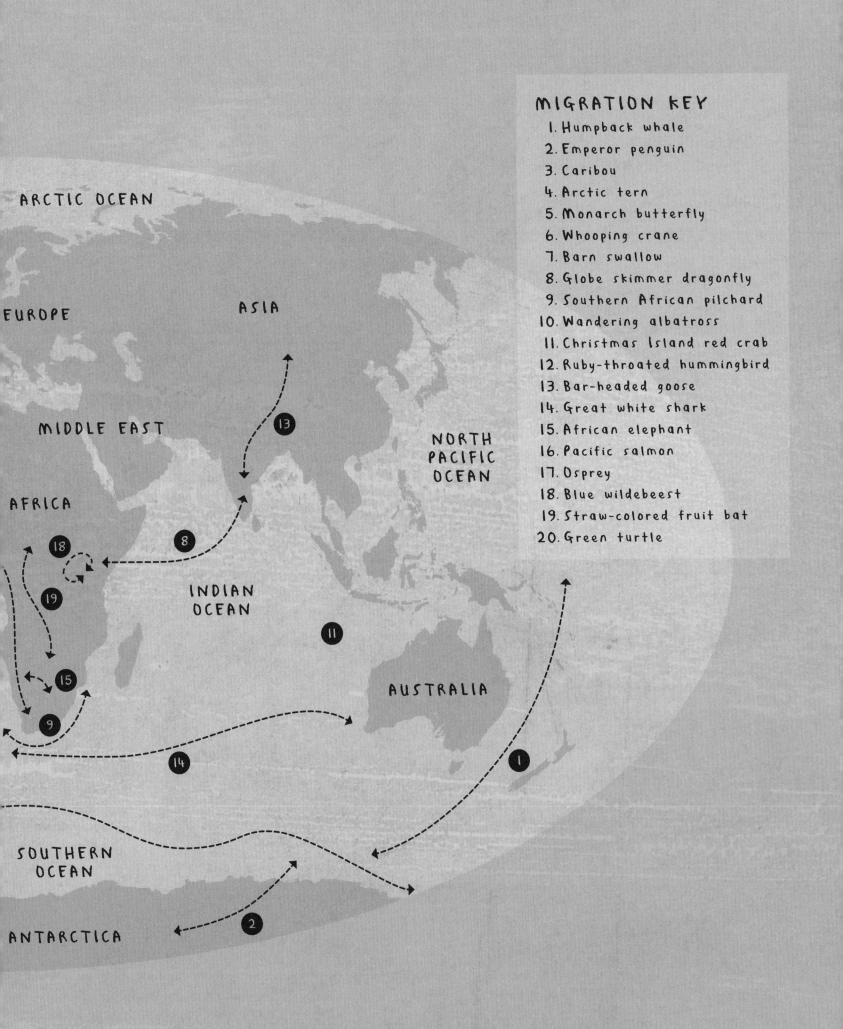

MIGRATION KEY
1. Humpback whale
2. Emperor penguin
3. Caribou
4. Arctic tern
5. Monarch butterfly
6. Whooping crane
7. Barn swallow
8. Globe skimmer dragonfly
9. Southern African pilchard
10. Wandering albatross
11. Christmas Island red crab
12. Ruby-throated hummingbird
13. Bar-headed goose
14. Great white shark
15. African elephant
16. Pacific salmon
17. Osprey
18. Blue wildebeest
19. Straw-colored fruit bat
20. Green turtle

For my daughter Flo,
on all her wild journeys.
—M.U.

For my adventurous sister Gabby,
who lives 10,500 miles away.
—J.D.

BLOOMSBURY CHILDREN'S BOOKS
Bloomsbury Publishing Inc., part of Bloomsbury Publishing Plc
1385 Broadway, New York, NY 10018

BLOOMSBURY, BLOOMSBURY CHILDREN'S BOOKS, and the Diana logo
are trademarks of Bloomsbury Publishing Plc

First published in Great Britain in May 2018 by Bloomsbury Publishing Plc
Published in the United States of America in August 2019
by Bloomsbury Children's Books

Text copyright © 2018 by Mike Unwin
Illustrations copyright © 2018 by Jenni Desmond

Bloomsbury books may be purchased for business or promotional use. For information on bulk purchases please contact
Macmillan Corporate and Premium Sales Department at specialmarkets@macmillan.com

Library of Congress Cataloging-in-Publication Data
available upon request
ISBN 978-1-5476-0097-7 (hardcover)
ISBN 978-1-5476-0138-7 (e-book) • ISBN 978-1-5476-0264-3 (e-PDF)

Art created with watercolor, acrylic, ink, pencil, and pencil crayon
Typeset in Opal LT Pro and JenniDesmond
Book design by Claire Jones
Printed and bound in China by Leo Paper Products, Heshan, Guangdong
4 6 8 10 9 7 5 3

To find out more about our authors and books visit www.bloomsbury.com and sign up for our newsletters.